D0964980

THINGS TO DO NOW THAT YOU'RE 60

things to do no

GRAEME KENT   Illustrations by Robyn Neild

hat you're 60

spruce

contents

friends and family

Make a list of all the good things in your life. How high do friends and family come on the list? Use your energies to build on these important relationships.

Start including your friends and family in your plans more frequently. Instead of hosting a party at home, why not all go away on vacation?

Take nothing and no one for granted. Make sure that you have whittled down your friends to those you really value and who value you. Life is too short for yes men and superficial acquaintances.

Make your own set of "Happy Families" cards for your family, based on your long knowledge of its members—play your new game at family get-togethers.

Enlist the help of relatives and draw up a family map of your home area, marking places where interesting or unusual things have happened to members of your family.

Revisit the places where you were happy as a child.

It was only after fifteen years of working together that Laurel and Hardy started to spend time in each other's company— and only then did they realize how important their friendship was. Be sure you value your oldest friendships.

You are different things to different people. Make a list of who you are at the moment—spouse, colleague, parent, child, and so on. Don't spend too much time on any one aspect of your life.

Arrange an evening of bingo for your competitive companions.

What role do you play in your family at the moment—peacemaker, benevolent despot, silent partner? If you don't like your role, make steps to change it.

Because you are sixty, your friends and family may start looking to you as a source of wisdom and experience. Preserve the illusion—nod sagely and say little.

Form a gang of family and friends in your age group. Compile a charter of irresponsible activities among yourselves and try to carry out at least one activity a day.

With a couple of friends, draw up your own consumer's guide for all the restaurants in your area. It's a fantastic excuse to try new cuisines and spend time with like-minded bons vivants.

For fun, start a new family tradition, like taking your shoes off before family meals. When you overhear a younger relative explaining, "I've no idea why we do this, but we've always done it!" you'll know you've succeeded!

Hire a minivan and take a few close friends and relations to your favorite place, whether it's a restaurant, beach, or park. Aim to make it their favorite place by the end of the trip.

Take a party of friends to a charity fashion show and gossip shamelessly about the models and their outfits.

Treat yourself and a friend to a night in a five-star hotel. Order the best champagne and caviar, live like a diva for an evening.

For your next birthday, throw yourself an extravagant party. If you have particularly extrovert friends, make it fancy dress. You're never too old for a wild party.

Organize a disco dancing session for your energetic buddies.

Form a quiz team of friends with varying ages. You could offer to be the specialist on the 1960s and '70s...

Arrange a 1950s-themed party. Ask guests to wear 1950s clothes and dance to 1950s music.

With a friend, try to ride on at least one vehicle invented since you were born. These might include a hovercraft (1952); jet boat (1957); or snowmobile (1959).

Buy concert tickets for a popular band or artist from your youth. Relive the moment when you and your friends first fell in love with a rock star and swore to be groupies forever.

Go to a local court case with a friend or relative. Afterward, enjoy arguing with one another about the verdict.

Choose one of your favorite songs and record yourself singing it. Give copies to your friends and family and delight in their strained enthusiasm.

If you ever wanted a tattoo when you were younger, but were always forbidden, now's the time to get one!

Buy that pair of Manolo Blahniks you've always wanted. See which member of your family is the first to comment when you wear them with pride.

Start looking at your friends through fresh eyes. Which of them would you want to go white-water rafting with?

Decide which of your friends you can depend upon to give you an honest opinion. Stick pretty close to them when your ideas get too fanciful.

Delight in your friendships.
"It is a sweet thing, friendship, a dear balm
A happy and auspicious bird of calm..."
PERCY BYSSHE SHELLEY

*Plant a friendship garden. Find
out the favorite flower of each of
your friends and give up a part of
your garden to these plants.*

Record a humorous message
on your answerphone.

Tell people close to you what you hope to do in the years to come. Let them know how you hope to include them in your plans.

Take a younger friend to see a reissue of an old movie that you really love.

Find a friend you can be silent with, as well as talk with, and spend a sunny afternoon with them in a park.

As other friends and family members turn sixty, present them with a small scrapbook containing tributes and reminiscences from friends and relations.

Cherish your friends—new and old.
"The friendship between me and you I will not compare to a chain, for that rains might rust, or the falling tree might break."
WILLIAM PENN

Start an annual family newsletter and make yourself editor. Distribute the newsletter at Christmas by e-mail or in the mail.

See how many family members from near and far you can get to attend an annual party.

Think about all of the positive things friends and relations have said about you to your face over the years. Try to live up to them.

Remember that friends
and relations have been
and will remain the sheet
anchors in your life.
Try to return the favor.

Remember, you may still be a parent, sibling, or
friend, and will be cherished as such but with the
new, fantastic era of retirement approaching,
above all you owe it to yourself to be you.

Keep in touch with your
family by any means.

Hope to be remembered. Do something to make sure that you are.

Regard friendship at sixty as a refuge. "The bird a nest, The spider a web, Man friendship."

WILLIAM BLAKE

Make the most of your family connections as you grow older. LaVell Edwards, football coach at Brigham Young University, was one of fourteen children. He said that the university did not dare fire him, because his family bought so many tickets for each game!

Be welcoming. You now have the experience and confidence to deal with any situation. Show this in the open way you deal with people and events.

When necessary, show your friendship in times of need by walking in when everybody else is walking out.

Keep your friendships in good repair. The Romans regarded this as so important that they started every year with a special day on which old friends could become reconciled.

Make an elderly relative's day by paying them a surprise visit and spending the afternoon catching up.

Let your friends and family know that there are no longer any curfews in your life. You are game for anything at any time.

Chill out, learn to break habits once in a while, and see what new opportunities present themselves. You *can* teach an old dog new tricks.

Start trawling secondhand stores. You'll find them a source of imaginative and inexpensive gifts for friends and family.

Make a list of those friends and members of your family you have not seen for some time. You could e-mail them, but a letter or telephone call is much more personal.

Improve your domestic arrangements if they are proving irritating. In 1886, exasperated by the number of dishes broken in the kitchen by her family and servants, Mrs. Josephine Cochrane of Illinois retired to the garden woodshed and invented the first dishwashing machine.

Build on your successes. Never dwell on failures—it will only get you down.

Ask at the local library for books on retirement. Chat to friends who have retired. How do they deal with being sixty? Make a note of all the things they come up with that inspire you.

Work on your image—if you've always had the same hairstyle or been afraid to change your style of dress, why not consider breaking with tradition and trying a new look?

Help to teach a child in your family how to read.

Do everything you do in style.

Make a list of organizations you would like to join, then pick one and take steps to become a member.

Take your time making friends,
but when you have done so,
remain loyal.
"Be slow to fall into friendship,
but when thou art in, continue
firm and constant."
SOCRATES

Go through your list of long-held
likes and dislikes. Select one of
your likes that is so way-out that
you cannot believe that anyone
else could possibly be crazy
enough to share it with you.
Then look for someone who does.

If you can, incorporate both love and friendships in your life.
"Love is like the wild rose-briar,
Friendship like the holly-tree—
The holly is dark when the rose-briar blooms
But which will bloom most constantly?"
EMILY BRONTË

Share your hobbies and interests. Look for groups of like-minded people.

There are a lot of interesting people out there. Try to meet some of them, for example by joining a club in your neighborhood. Dr. Samuel Johnson said, "Sir, I look upon every day to be lost, in which I do not make a new acquaintance."

There are many criteria for selecting new friends, but the best is still the good old-fashioned gut feeling. Trust your instincts.

Make friends of as many different ages as possible. If you want to be, you can be the sage mentor to the young, and the giddy, irresponsible youth to those older than you are.

Find out the birthdays of new friends and send them cards—and always remember your old friends' birthdays.

Don't worry if some of your new friends are unlike any you have had before. When the drama critic James Agate was asked, in his fifties, why he spent so much time with a rather eccentric musician, he replied, "His nonsense suits my nonsense."

Learn to listen more to friends and family.
"A bore is a person who talks when you want him to listen."
AMBROSE BIERCE

If your children are leaving home, let go and be proud of them. They are entitled to a life too.

It's sad when a child leaves home, but look at the positives—an extra bedroom to do with what you will! Turn it into a studio for painting or a study for writing that long-awaited first novel.

It's hard to clear out your child's room. Try not to be too ruthless. Keep those irreplaceable items that bring back memories even if you have to add an extra bedroom in which to house them!

Write a letter to your children telling them the single most important thing you have learned now you are sixty.

Don't get rid of your children's toys; your grandchildren will be fascinated by their simple rustic antiquity and the fact that they used to belong to "Mom" or "Dad" (and you will finally get a chance to master the rules of Ludo).

When your children leave home, regard it as a gap year, not a permanent absence. They will return.

Continue to involve your children in your life. Take your children into your confidence. Talk to them about how you want your life to change.

Surprise your children— ask them for their advice.

Learn a new skill: putting yourself first. Reassert the right to be first in line when it comes to deciding who gets the family car for the day.

You may have a second crack at parenthood by proxy if you become a grandparent. What can you learn from your experiences with your children that will make you a better grandparent?

Incorporate your grandchildren, at a suitable level, in any keep-fit program you are undergoing. Take them for walks and play tag and Frisbee with them in the park. They will help you to feel young.

Refuse to be typecast. It's perfectly possible to be a highly successful grandparent and sexy with it.

When your children become parents, enjoy watching them make the transition from the nurtured to the nurturing.

Help your children by shouldering your share of the plethora of unpaid tasks for grandparents. According to a survey carried out in 2004, 49 percent of grandparents babysat regularly and more than 25 percent help with gardening and household repairs.

Make each grandchild feel special by having one special and particular day dedicated to each one. Plan an outing or activity to spoil your grandchild and yourself.

Be brave under pressure. Remember the great pleasure of being a grandparent—you get to hand the children back at the end of the day.

Start putting together your own collection of children's bedtime stories—ones you have heard, read, or made up yourself. Reading these stories will be an event that you all look forward to and your appreciative audience will be spellbound by your storytelling skill!

Be a safe pair of hands for the whole family, ready to pick everyone up and dust them down. They will appreciate your support and repay it ten-fold.

Respect any rules that your children have made for their children. Don't spoil your grandchildren (too much) or undermine your child's authority as a parent.

When your grandchildren are old enough, instigate a weekly phone call for a free-ranging chat, with no parents allowed! It's great fun.

Relinquish family responsibilities with grace. The time will come, if it has not already, when your children will want to take over the planning of family get-togethers.

If you want to go on a Caribbean cruise at Christmas instead of spending it with your adult children, don't feel guilty: just do it.

Work on that family tree you have always wanted to draw up. There are many Web sites and computer programs that will help you to get started.

Use your family tree as the basis for the writing of a family history. Gather anecdotes from relatives about grandparents, great-aunts, and great-uncles.

Before you embark on a family vacation, employ tact, sensitivity, and forethought.

Get hold of a camcorder and start making a filmed record of your family.

If you enjoy editing videos, borrow family footage from different members of the family and edit them into one definitive family record.

If the technical side of camcorders and video editing is a foreign land, use this as an opportunity to enlist the aid of younger family members, and get to know them better at the same time.

Borrow any written records—diaries and letters—that relatives are prepared to let you have. Put them in secure folders and store them for generations to come.

Keep local newspaper clippings containing mentions of family members, no matter how fleeting or trivial. You'll be glad you did.

Ask older relatives to write brief accounts of special days in their lives, such as their first day at school, first job, wedding, etc.

If you find that one particular family member has a really interesting history, prepare a special account of his or her life—make a video, put together a scrapbook—and present it to them as a gift at a birthday or celebration.

Prepare a timeline, with events from your family history above the line, and national and international events below it. Present your collection to the rest of your family. It's always a thrill to learn about family history.

Now that you have started to voyage through your family's history, use your discoveries to find out more about yourself. Use your record-gathering as an opportunity to assess your own role in the family over the last sixty years.

Always listen to friends and relations who warn you that you are doing too much. They may be right.

activities
and hobbies

Never stop listening to your inner child. "A man at sixteen will prove a child at sixty."
EIGHTEENTH-CENTURY PROVERB

> Let me be a free man.
> Free to travel. Free to stop.
> Free to work. Free to choose my own teachers.
> Free to follow the religion of my fathers.
> Free to think and talk and act for myself.
> CHIEF JOSEPH, NEZ PERCÉ TRIBE,
> SPEAKING IN HIS FIFTIES

Value and cherish the past, but don't be trapped by it. Now is the time to look forward to the future.

Look back over the last few years and decide which parts of your life you have enjoyed the most. Devote more time to them over the next few years.

Have great ambitions—and attempt to carry some of them out. It may be too late to start a fashion empire, but you could start making clothes for yourself and look into supplying garments for local boutiques.

"As one grows older, one climbs with surprising strides."
GEORGE SAND

Fulfill a flippant ambition. Aspirations don't have to be significant.

"I always wondered what I would look like in uniform, so I volunteered to spend Saturday evenings as a doorman at the local community center. The only drawback was that there was only one uniform and the doorman before me was four inches taller than I am."
RETIRED DOCK WORKER

Construct a sign saying, "Leisure Is As Important As Work" and hang it somewhere prominent as a reminder to yourself.

Hunt around for all the leisure-time projects you have abandoned over the years. Now's your chance to pick up where you left off.

Join a retirement group and make new friends to be lazy with.

George Bidder invented the railway swing bridge, but he was also immensely proud of his ability to do calculations in his head. In his fifties and early sixties, long after he had given up inventing, he would appear in public to give demonstrations of mental arithmetic.

Polish up on any talents that you have, or find new ones by taking up a new hobby.

Be prepared to lose yourself in your hobbies. Devote one day of every week to doing a creative hobby when no one can disturb you and you forget about all those chores that need doing.

"Old age is like everything else. To make a success of it you've got to start young."

FRED ASTAIRE

Draw on your experiences, no matter how bad they may have seemed at the time.

Prepare for your new life of new activity by doing some research. Get acquainted with the Internet and find out what clubs and events are around in your neighborhood.

Try going to an art gallery instead of washing the car on a Sunday afternoon. It's amazing how rejuvenating it is to dispense with long-standing rituals.

> When Time who steals our years away
> Shall steal our pleasures too,
> The mem'ry of the past will stay
> And half our joys renew.

THOMAS MOORE

Get accustomed to the idea that your time is your own. Don't let anyone take it away from you.

> The true way to render age vigorous is to prolong the youth of the mind.
>
> MORTIMER COLLINS

Preserve the youth of your mind by seeing if you can name three actors from one of your favorite TV shows from the 1960s.

Most of us do our best work in the mornings. Now is the time to prepare for a productive retirement by shifting more and more decision-making activities to before noon.

Try something new every day and you might like some of them enough to incorporate them in your future plans.

Turn the complaint "I wish I could" into the mantra "I can."

Find role models in your age group who have gone off to try something new, exciting, and different. Aim to become a role model yourself.

Think seriously about the ways in which you wish to spend your retirement. Most people when questioned want to spend this time engaged in meaningful, useful activities, not relaxing.

You've worked hard for years. Now it's time to play hard.

> " It's not the years in your life that count. It's the life in your years. "
>
> ABRAHAM LINCOLN

There's always more to learn, no matter how much you think you know. Why don't you start taking evening classes?

Be selective in your choices. Before long you will be so busy you will wonder how you ever found time to go to work.

A new life is waiting for you. Don't be surprised if you find it in some unusual places.

" Twenty years from now you will be more disappointed by the things that you didn't do than by the ones that you did. "
MARK TWAIN

Regard your new life as a game of bridge—know when and what to discard.

Earn money, make friends, and learn a language. Approach local colleges and offer to give board and lodging to an overseas student.

You've spent a lifetime learning. Put it to good use and enter local quiz competitions, or try to complete more difficult crosswords.

Take advantage of technology. As actress Honor Blackman, still working well after her sixtieth year, says, "Life has become much easier for women…With supermarkets and washing machines and Hoovers women were freed to get on with life, and found they still had energy."

Brush up on your jigsaw puzzle techniques. Always start by putting the four corner pieces in place, then assemble the sides. Only bend a piece out of shape as a last resort or at the height of frustration!

Save money by going to the hairdresser or barber on senior citizens' days (but remember that you might find some old people there!)

Life gets cheaper as you get older — try not to be too smug when you're checking out the concessions!

Don't throw your guitar and your musical ambitions away. Be daring and form a musical group. You've got more life experience to pour into musical creativity now than when you were a kid.

There isn't a vast audience for Elvis Presley imitators but that needn't prevent you from polishing your version of "Blue Suede Shoes." If you can't find an audience, buy a full-length mirror to perform in front of.

Get your dancing shoes out—ask a teenager from your family to teach you a completely new dance. You might surprise yourself.

Go to a "tribute band" concert and reminisce about the days when music was "proper" music.

Go the whole hog and become a groupie on a "golden oldies" tour.

If you don't already do so, start listening to the radio again. Take part in a phone-in on a subject you're passionate about instead of shouting your views at the radio in vain.

Stretch yourself. Write the words and music for a musical. Then get together with friends to put on a performance.

Learn to play a musical instrument. There are hundreds of "Late Starter" orchestras around the world.

Start buying old singalong records from secondhand stores.

Invent a new cocktail, made up of your favorite ingredients. Give it a name that's in tune with your age and ambitions, such as "Fall Surprise." After all, if you can't enjoy an afternoon cocktail now…

Wallow in nostalgia. Visit a bar that you frequented as a youngster and check out how much it has changed.

While you're out on the town, test the barman's cocktail expertise.

Rediscover the joys of the afternoon snooze.

Start going to the cinema occasionally in the afternoon. After a lifetime of work, it is one of the most deliciously decadent of pastimes.

Watch old black and white movies with stars you've almost forgotten...in the afternoon, with the curtains drawn.

Watch an old movie called *The Judge Steps Out* (1949), starring and co-written by Alexander Knox. It's an inspirational story of a judge who suddenly abandons his old life and heads off into the wide blue yonder.

Make a list of your top ten films and find the time to watch them.

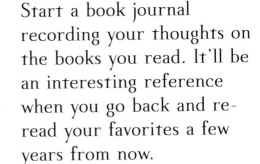

Re-read a favorite book. Start a book journal recording your thoughts on the books you read. It'll be an interesting reference when you go back and re-read your favorites a few years from now.

> "Let those who
> would write heroic
> poems make their
> life an heroic poem."
> JOHN MILTON

Devise and maintain a
good family filing system.

In the lead-up to his sixtieth birthday, author Norman Mailer read over a hundred books on ancient Egypt while researching for his novel Ancient Evenings. *Find a subject that fascinates you and research it thoroughly.*

Read *Bright Day*, by J. B. Priestley. It is a wonderful novel about a writer who returns, in his imagination, to the halcyon days of his youth just before the outbreak of World War I.

Another great novel to read about the importance of memories of the past is A Breeze of Morning, *by Charles Morgan. It is the story of a boy's first love, recollected many years later.*

If you've always wanted to write a novel, this is the time to do it. Draw on your experiences and you'll be halfway there.

It is said that experience recollected in tranquillity can be a great spur. Make a collection of your most interesting memories.

Make sure that you have lots of happy memories. Quiz those who have known you over the years and ask for their recollections.

" Some books seem to have been written not to teach us anything, but to let us know that the author has known something. "
JOHANN WOLFGANG VON GOETHE

Try your hand at writing poetry then submit your best example to one of the hundreds of poetry competitions in existence.

Start small. The shortest poem in existence is said to be the anonymous:
"Adam
Had 'em."
Can you find, or write, a shorter poem?

Help improve your writing and at the same time get organized: start a diary.

After a few weeks, assess your diary—look at the occasions that you enjoyed and those that you didn't. It's a good way of making the way you spend your time more positive and pleasurable to yourself.

66 When I retired, my wife said that she supposed I would now realize my ambition to take up golf. I never remembered having any such ambition! I think she just wanted to get me out from under her feet. 99

RETIRED OFFICE WORKER

Don't take up activities deemed suitable for your age unless you really want to. Expand your horizons—if you want to get into surfing, go for it.

Celebrate your birthday by walking a mile a day for each year of your life.

Wade in at least four different seas or oceans.

Start looking for esoteric sports that someone of sixty can win by years of carefully developed cunning, rather than by youthful ability.

This could also be the time to start considering fishing as a hobby. It may be the one activity in which you can sit staring aimlessly into space and people will still respect your privacy.

Amateur athletic associations are desperately short of officials—judges, timekeepers, starters, and so on. Brush up on the rules and get involved: it's much more fun than yelling at the TV when officials make a questionable decision.

Take up debating, breadmaking, mah-jongg, chess, salsa, or high board diving—don't just stick to the tennis club.

Plan to sit in your garden and enjoy it as often as you work in it. "Nothing so pleasant as to sit amid that mixture of flower and leaf, watching the bee-bird. Nothing so pretty as my garden."

MARY RUSSELL MITFORD

Experiment with a miniature garden. Use a corner of your real garden, or a container indoors, and try different layouts. You could try a bonsai garden with dwarf trees, or a mini rock garden, with various stones and alpine plants.

Start raising plants for charity sales. Attractive, easy-to-nurture plants include sweet peas, pansies, and stocks.

Plant a tree to announce your sixtieth year. Grow with it.

Start a sketchbook. Make sketches of scenes that attract you. When you have more time, turn these sketches into paintings. This is the perfect time of life to become an artist: you have experience, freedom, and wisdom on your side.

Surprise yourself: learn about art history, music, ballet, or theater and see how much you can get out of it.

Choose a particular geological formation, natural phenomenon, or landscape feature that interests you—such as caves, waterfalls, and so on. Visit appropriate sites and take photos, then compile a photographic album.

Keep doing what you like doing.

There must be a lot of places you haven't visited for a long time. Schedule an itinerary that will involve returning to your old haunts.

Go beachcombing.

With some like-minded enthusiasts, hire a luxury car for a day.

Start looking at your town through fresh eyes. Pretend that you are a tourist. What can you find out about your own area? See what the local reference library can do to help.

Indulge—spend a day shopping.

Know when to be silent.

Some of our contact with others takes the form of nonverbal communication. Discover what your own posture and movement say about you.

Make a list of the people you get on well with. Why do you get on with them? Can you use this information to discover how to deal with other people you meet?

Most schools are crying out for senior citizens who are prepared to supplement the History curriculum by talking to children about life fifty years ago. Don't throw away those old photographs. Put them aside and start polishing your anecdotes ready for the day when you become an example of Living History.

There are plenty of youth organizations that are desperate for leaders and helpers. Go and share your experience and get a whole new perspective on life.

Practice saying "No." There may be many demands on your time and talents. Make people give you exact details of what they want from you before you decide to take on any new activities.

Start thinking about having a pet. Pet-owners have lower stress levels than the occupants of animal-free homes. Stroking a cat or dog is highly therapeutic. If you love walking, get a dog—if you are a homebody, relax with a cat.

Consider keeping fish as a hobby. Gazing at fish is known to be incredibly calming. Start with freshwater fish, as they are easier to look after.

Local amateur dramatic societies are always on the lookout for enthusiastic new members. Attend one of the society's performances and offer your services afterward. If, in addition, you can offer backstage skills such as carpentry or lighting, they should fall upon you with glee.

Steel yourself, mentally and physically, to sort out the accumulated junk and treasures in the attic. Be selective. To date there have been no significant price offers recorded for plastic dishes. There probably isn't a great market for old Frisbees either. Earmark them for the trash can.

Turn unwanted items into cash by selling them. To ensure maximum profits, wait (if possible) for five years before reselling anything of value.

Now is the time to start developing any collections that you may once have started. Study newspaper advertisements and look for auctions and garage sales for bargains.

Study www.ebay.com, the Internet auction site. There's a whole new world out there to enjoy from the comfort of your sitting room.

A popular, if time-consuming, hobby to take up is that of searching for buried treasure using a metal detector.

You can search for treasure without a metal detector: the seashore, after the tide has gone out, is a good place for finds. Make sure that you have taken all possible safety precautions and know the movement and times of incoming tides.

Just because you have reached sixty, it does not mean that your new hobbies have to be staid—far from it! Follow the examples of other retirees and preretirees and opt for more unusual pastimes.

Start a society for the preservation of sidewalks. Children will love to join you jumping over any cracks in the paving stones!

Eat out as much as possible and broaden your appreciation of foreign food.

nurturing the
outer you

> Look to your health and if you have it, praise God, and value it next to a good conscience.
>
> IZAAC WALTON

Note the three main components of fitness—flexibility, strength, and stamina. Look for enjoyable activities that will enhance your quota of each.

Give yourself a thorough medical checkup even if you think there is nothing wrong with you.

Take a fresh look at your lifestyle and assess where things need to change. Are you eating your five portions of fruit and vegetables a day?

Look after yourself, but enjoy yourself in the process.
"The best doctors in the world are Dr. Diet, Dr. Quiet, and Dr. Merryman."
JONATHAN SWIFT

A Japanese study of people's diet in their later years indicated that the fittest and healthiest subjects were those who ate only until they were about 80 percent full. Consider adopting this as a maxim.

Stimulate your taste buds by eating hot and cold foods at the same meal—what was that about older people losing their taste ability?

If you have avoided the water bandwagon all these years, get on it now. The health benefits of drinking plenty of water every day are numerous.

Plan your own dietary improvements and avoid faddy diets.

Spur on your metabolism and eat five small meals a day, rather than three big ones.

Cut down on fatty foods and reduce your intake of salt and sugar to give your metabolism a head start.

If you are unhappy with your weight, do something about it! Have a realistic goal—aim to shed two or three pounds a month if you can.

Take heed of the old adage, "Breakfast like a king, lunch like a prince, and dine like a pauper." Make breakfast the most exciting meal of the day—why not try some new exotic fruits?

Get a medical checkup that assesses your pulse rate, cholesterol level, lung capacity, blood pressure, vision, and hearing.

No excuses—start exercising right now! Research shows that people over fifty-five who exercised sensibly improved their strength and fitness as effectively as those in their twenties and thirties.

If you have got stairs in your house or apartment block, climb them every day, as often and as quickly as you can. Getting out of breath at least once a day helps to strengthen the heart and improve the circulation.

Kill two birds with one stone: incorporate everyday activities such as gardening, maintenance, and housework into your exercise plan.

If you don't already have a green thumb, take up gardening and turn your backyard into that blooming haven of tranquillity you have always wanted it to be.

Turn your hand to bonsai and discover a most therapeutic and creative hobby.

Join a gentle aerobics class with a small group of friends. Exercising to music is both enjoyable and effective and having friends around makes the experience much less daunting.

Ensure that there are suitable muscle-building exercises, such as push-ups, in your aerobic workout. This will compensate for any muscle-loss and will also help to keep your weight down.

Perform exercises that test your balance, such as walking along straight lines on the floor, to help guard against falls in later life.

Go for a weekly walk with a friend of your own age. You'll get some gentle exercise, have a chance to catch up on the gossip, and occasionally it's good to have someone to help you home!

Consider taking up a new sport or active pastime. Try something you would never have considered before, such as surfing or rollerblading.

A walk is one of the secrets for dodging old age.
RALPH WALDO EMERSON

Walking staves off heart disease, reduces the risk of high blood pressure, improves muscle tone, fights back pain, and guards against respiratory problems. Start gently and build up to 30 minutes' walking a day.

Time yourself over a 1-mile walk. Repeat the walk every day and time yourself at monthly intervals to watch your progress.

Leave your car in its garage. A survey has shown that city dwellers who regularly walk to stores are on average six pounds lighter than suburbanites who usually drive to malls.

Start getting off public transport two stops before your intended destination.

Embark upon a regime of swimming training. Swimming exercises the muscles, lungs, and heart. It also develops suppleness, strength, and stamina without placing undue strain on the body.

Try to find a local swimming pool that offers the pool exclusively to senior swimmers at certain times of day, or at least provides a roped-off section of the pool for them.

Undertake simple aerobic exercises in the local swimming pool. The water will take the stress off your joints. To start with, exercise in waist-deep water. As you grow stronger and fitter, move to water at chest level. This will provide even more resistance.

Archery is an attractive hobby for both men and women and helps to develop physical strength, and hand to eye coordination. Find an archery club to join.

If you're not tempted to take up what you consider to be cliched retirement pastimes, grab the bull by the horns and try your hand at extreme ironing. This increasingly popular craze sees people hanging from clifftops performing a once mundane household chore.

Spend an evening with the youngsters in your family and take them tenpin bowling. It's a great sport for people of all ages.

Taking up golf at sixty is a bit of a cliché, but pay no heed to that. It will get you out in the fresh air, make you walk, and increase your coordination.

Make golf an excuse to socialize, and arrange regular games with different friends. You can play top-class golf to quite a late age.

Learn to dance, particularly those dances involving groups—folk, country, line dancing—where you will meet more people of your own age.

Take up bell-ringing. You could have a swinging time and it will exercise muscles you never knew you had!

Explore the possibilities of the ancient Indian art of yoga. This develops the body's physical, emotional, and spiritual aspects through movement, control of the will and emotions, and meditation.

If you have no pets of your own, now is the time to think about getting a dog. Or why not offer to walk your neighbor's dog?

Cycling provides excellent exercise for the legs and heart. Start by cycling short distances on traffic-free routes, and work up to three longer sessions a week.

If you are feeling adventurous, consider taking up horseracing. John Thorne, a grandfather, came second in the 1981 English Grand National riding a horse named Spartan Missile.

Join a golf club, or a rowing, fencing, or pole vaulting club!

Consider using an inflatable gym ball for simple exercises, such as stomach crunches and stretches. The ball provides support for joints and back.

You may already be fitter than you think—if your training in any sport is progressing well, think about entering veterans' events at local clubs.

*Launch a campaign to have
the 50-meter sprint classified
as a middle-distance event!*

Consider the advantages of the ancient
Chinese art of tai chi, a series of exercises
designed to combat stress and fatigue,
improve flexibility, and encourage
harmony between mind and body.

*Find a really obscure sport
and become very good at it.*

By all means try cross-country skiing, but start in a small country!

Adopt any form of exercise that takes your fancy. Cardinal Richlieu, the greatest and busiest figure in seventeenth-century France, exercised daily by jumping over pieces of furniture.

Take up horse-riding. Riding with friends in the countryside can be very peaceful and relaxing.

Try a competitive sport. Getting a little competitive gets your adrenaline going and keeps the activity exciting and engaging.

Glory in your age. In the 2004 San Diego Senior Olympics, one of the soccer teams called itself "Vintage," while another, even more down-to-earth, entered as "Old as Dirt."

As early as the eighteenth century, poet John Dryden appreciated that outdoor pursuits were more effective than doctors' surgeries for people as they grew older.

"Better hunt in fields for health unbought,
Than fee the doctor for a nauseous draught,
The wise, for cure, on exercise depend,
God never made his work for man to mend."

JOHN DRYDEN

Be optimistic about the level of sporting achievement you will attain.

Strive to reverse the ageing process. Peter Z. Cohen, a professor of orthopedic surgery with thirty years' experience, studied the progress of many older athletes and stated, "Aerobic exercise can make your heart as efficient at age sixty as the heart of a sedentary person who is twenty-five years old."

"Start low and go slow!" This is the advice of Miriam C. Morey of the Veteran Affairs Medical Center in Durham, North Carolina, to those older people taking up an exercise regime.

To aid relaxation (especially after all your sporting efforts), enroll on a course of acupuncture.

Adopt flexible bedtimes, and don't go to bed until you are tired. Make sure that your mattress is comfortable and the bedroom dark and well-ventilated.

Ward off insomnia. Avoid caffeine after mid-afternoon and put several drops of lavender oil on a tissue on your pillow. The vapors are soothing and relaxing, and encourage restful sleep.

Enjoy your lie-ins. "The happiest part of a man's life is what he passes lying awake in bed in the morning."

SAMUEL JOHNSON

Take heart—you've still got sex-appeal. Actor Sean Connery was sixty years old when he was nominated by Playboy magazine as the world's sexiest man. "It'll be all downhill from here," he sighed.

Take an early morning ride on a tandem bicycle with your partner. Cycle in a leafy park or down country roads and bask in the peace of a new day.

You don't need top-quality fitness and athleticism to take up bridge, but it is one of the best mental activities, demanding that the player develops considerable mathematical ability and memory retention. Find a bridge club and buff up those brain cells in convivial company.

One of the most rewarding games for people in their sixties is bowls. Many small towns have at least one club.

Spend time improving your fitness and well-being—start walking regularly with friends or a partner. Plan to go for a walk and reward yourself with a picnic at the end of it.

exploring the
inner you

Be proud of your maturity, don't deny it.

Throw away any preconceived inhibitions and forget your chronological age. In retirement, you'll have the opportunity to be an absolute beginner at some of the new things you undertake.

Don't feel trapped in your life. Now is the time to break out and try something new.

"Men seek out retreats for themselves in the country, by the seaside, on the mountains... But all this is unphilosophical to the last degree...when thou canst at a moment's notice retire into thyself."

MARCUS AURELIUS

Put aside time for reflection and dreaming. You are about to enter into a very busy and productive time in your life and you will need to be able to take a step back every now and again.

Spend a little time remembering all the people who have helped you over the course of your life so far. Consider writing an appreciative note to those who have particularly touched you.

Explore this formula for achieving inner peace and satisfaction as you grow older: seek to have something to do, something to strive for, and someone to love.

Use your experience to seek equilibrium in your life at this important stage. Think, feel, believe, and act.

Enjoy each moment. Your experience will have told you by now that good things do not always last, so make the most of each enjoyable event until the next one comes along, as it surely will.

In 2004, Howard and Marika Stone, who operate the Too Young to Retire Web site (www.2young2retire.com), organized a competition to find a better name for retirement. The winner was "Renaissance," signifying an awakening or rebirth.

Look to the future. We have all accumulated baggage. The trick is not to keep unpacking it.

 Retirement is essentially your time. Get used to being good to yourself and putting yourself first for a change.

Retirement also means breaking your routine. Start preparing for new events, even if it only entails reading a different newspaper.

Refuse to conform to stereotypes of age. You are you.

Just now and again, surprise your nearest and dearest by doing something out of character.

Don't avoid problems. Every time you successfully solve one, it will increase your confidence and self-esteem.

Work at self-improvement, whether you're tackling trivial things or bigger soul-searching issues.

66 *There are glimpses of heaven to us in every act, or thought, or word that raises us above ourselves.* 99
ARTHUR P. STANLEY

Plan to make your next year a voyage of self-discovery. Embark upon your journey with enthusiasm. Be prepared to be flexible—mentally as well as physically.

" Wheresoever you go, go with all your heart. "

CONFUCIUS

Work on your tolerance levels. See how long you can go in a day without judging anyone.

Be aware of the wisdom and experience of others, but only insofar as these will help you choose your own path.

" Do not go where the path may lead, go instead where there is no path and leave a trail. "

RALPH WALDO EMERSON

Reflect upon your recent actions and thoughts. Can you discern patterns in your actions and reactions to situations?

Consider how your personality is projected to other people. If you were another person, would you like the current you?

Write down five words to describe yourself as if you were someone else analyzing your personality.

Don't be afraid to make changes to yourself, whether on a superficial level or in the murky depths of personality and behavior.

> " As human beings, our greatness lies not so much in being able to remake the world…as in being able to remake ourselves. "
>
> MAHATMA GANDHI

Have some of your reactions to situations become too automatic? Try to take each new situation as it comes. Reflect upon your alternatives before deciding on a course of action.

Retain a sense of humor when things go wrong. Succeed in this, and you will always have a smile on your face, no matter what life throws at you.

Work on your self-esteem. Confidence in all that you do is the key to feeling good about yourself.

Remember to look back and appreciate what you have done in your life. Don't waste time regretting what you haven't done.

What have you done so far that you think is particularly interesting or unusual? Decide what made these events valuable. They do not have to be earth-shaking events: make a list of matters that were important to you.

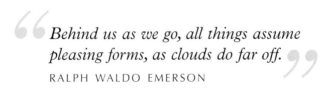

Behind us as we go, all things assume pleasing forms, as clouds do far off.

RALPH WALDO EMERSON

Decide which attributes you have developed over the years. What use can you make of your strengths now you are sixty?

Bear in mind that you are unique. "All the knowledge I possess everyone else can acquire, but my heart is all my own."

JOHANN WOLFGANG VON GOETHE

Remember that it is a good thing to think deeply, but not to the exclusion of all else. As Oliver Edwards said, "I have tried too in my time to be a philosopher, but, I don't know how, cheerfulness was always breaking in."

Take time to study everything you see. Look for its inner and outer beauty. The artist John Constable said, "I never saw an ugly thing in my life: for let the form of an object be what it may— light, shade, and perspective will always make it beautiful."

Put any bad memories firmly behind you.
"I sit beside my lonely fire,
And pray for wisdom yet
For calmness to remember
Or courage to forget."
CHARLES AIDE

In 1894, humorist Mark Twain was almost sixty and contemplating bankruptcy. He was a poor businessman and had lost most of his money in the invention of a typesetting machine, which had failed. Twain refused to be dispirited. "Take heart," he wrote (tongue in cheek) to his beloved wife, "the worst is yet to come." He was forced into bankruptcy but settled down, in his sixties, to a feverish regime of writing and within a few years had paid off all his creditors in full, although legally he was not forced to do so. "Honor," he explained simply, "is a harder master than the law."

Show a cheerful face to the world: optimism has been proved to provide resilience and induce the feeling of being in charge of situations. On the other hand, do not be foolhardily cheerful. Borrowing from the words of the poet Rudyard Kipling, if you can keep your head while all about you are losing theirs, you probably don't appreciate the true facts of the situation. Temper optimism with common sense.

Smile. It reduces stress. The physical act prompts the mind to release chemicals that trigger pleasant emotions.

Remember the words of the comedian Charlie Chester, who said: "Keeping up appearances is one thing; keeping up your spirits is everything."

With your incipient change in lifestyle you may find yourself in charge of groups, such as committees or voluntary organizations, for the first time. Study how to motivate people. Try to work out what makes different people tick: is it pride, money, companionship, or gratitude?

Keep in mind that there is a time for boldness.
"Whatever you can do or dream, you can begin it.
Boldness has genius, power, and magic in it.
Begin it now."
JOHANN WOLFGANG VON GOETHE

Practice motivating yourself. If you are about to perform an uncongenial task, promise yourself a stipulated treat at its successful conclusion.

Take the time to encourage others. It will make you feel good about yourself and people will appreciate your time and energy.

Always be the initiator— try not to go with the tide.

Tune in to your emotions, but don't be governed by them.

Communicate. When you understand yourself, seek to be understood by others.

Be specific in your intentions. Break challenges down into their smallest possible components and the task will become far less daunting.

Remember that you must make the final choices about your life yourself. Don't rely on your partner or friends to push you in a particular direction and hope it all turns out for the best.

Live by this advice from a senior British politician. "[There are] three questions to ask before a period of change: 'What is going on?' 'Why is it going on?' 'What can I do about it?'"

ANTHONY WEDGWOOD BENN

Take risks. Live a little. Strike up a conversation with a cute guy sitting next to you on the subway. You might come away with a new friend and an ego boost.

Revisit your spiritual side. If you've never given much thought to God or any Supreme Being, decide what place a supreme being has in your life.

Work out what your values are and adhere to them. This will give you self-confidence and help you to adopt the right attitude. In turn, this will empower your behavior.

Arrange to spend more time with people who love, cherish, and value you. Your self-esteem and mood will soar.

Consider the eight noble truths of Buddhism: right knowledge, right attitude, right speech, right action, right living, right effort, right mindfulness, and right composure.

When the time for thinking is over, the time for putting beliefs into action will have come. Take inspiration from the great leader Gandhi, who said, "My life is my message."

Meditate. Sit comfortably for twenty minutes, concentrating on your breathing to the exclusion of all else. Drive all thoughts from your mind and enjoy the tranquillity of this, your own personal time. "He who lives in harmony with himself lives in harmony with the universe."
MARCUS AURELIUS

Keep mentally alert. Put aside time for crossword puzzles and games such as chess, bridge, and Scrabble.

Nurture your memory. A very useful exercise lies in the practice of mnemonics—using verses and initials to recall subjects, for example. Buy a book explaining how to improve your memory and avoid becoming absent-minded as you get older.

Strive to do many things, but be sure to concentrate and remain focused on only one thing at a time to get the most from it.

Two great aids to retaining mental agility are generally held to be creativity and concentration. Try to use them in combination—for example in painting, a hobby that can be taken up at any age.

Further your education and broaden your mind. Enroll on a part-time course at a local college.

Make plans to read all the books you have always wanted to read. Ask at your local public library about readers' discussion groups in your area.

career and lifestyle

Make some decisions about what you really want out of life. "A lifestyle is what you pay for; a life is what pays you."
THOMAS LEONARD

Remain in contact with others. No matter how engrossing your hobby or work, social interaction with others is an essential factor in maintaining mental and physical alertness.

Whatever your age, think very carefully before deciding to retire. If you are enjoying your work and are in good health, consider staying on.

Well in advance of retirement, sort out your financial situation. Get forecasts of pensions and annuities. Study interest rates on savings.

Write down your daily expenses and see if you can cut back on unnecessary spending. Put aside what you save in a savings account and treat yourself to a vacation in a year's time.

Before you retire, work out what you will be saving in workplace expenses—the cost of travel, meals, clothing, and so on. Balance this against the reduction in your income.

Are you happy with your job? Don't stick out your remaining working years in a job you cannot stand. It's not too late to find work that you enjoy.

If you are approaching your company's mandatory retirement age and would prefer to continue working, have a word with your boss. You may be surprised at how much he wants you to stay on. The thought of training your replacement may be filling him with dread.

If you have decided to leave your job, offer to take over the training of your successor. It's the perfect opportunity to become a mentor or even a role model.

If the thought of a work-free retirement fills you with dread, check out the opportunities for returning to your old workplace as a consultant, or as a temporary staff member to provide cover when full-time staff are on vacation.

Ask your boss and senior colleagues if they would be prepared to write references for you if you decide to apply for other jobs.

If you can't decide whether to work on or to pursue your interests, try both.

Make a list of the jobs (voluntary or paid) that you would like to try. Remember Maxim Gorky's adage, "When work is a pleasure, life is a joy. When work is a duty, life is slavery!"

Don't worry if you can't break in at the top level of your preferred new field. Compromise. For example, you may not get a job with a national broadcaster, but hospital radio stations welcome volunteers.

Take a vocational guidance test. It could be money well spent and it's never too late to learn about yourself. Use the results to help find a new job that fits you like a glove.

Reassess your personality. Do you think you are a leader or a follower? What difference will this make in any change of lifestyle on your part?

Join a few clubs and societies and strive to make contacts and new friends. You never know what opportunities might present themselves at your next bridge club evening.

Some of the strong points of older workers are stability, reliability, commitment, responsibility, and maturity. How do you stack up in these areas?

If you can afford it, consider taking up a franchise which involves hiring the name, expertise, and services of a national organization.

Consider developing a hobby into a second career.

If you can't beat 'em, join 'em! A 1994 survey indicated that one growth industry of the future would be that of catering for an ageing population. Don't let the kids muscle in. Start your own business catering for your peers.

*Learn from your last job.
What were your strengths and
what could you have done better?*

Start updating your CV. Hopefully a lot has happened to you since you last looked at it. Include sections on strengths, qualifications, experience, interests, skills, and hobbies. You never know what dream job is waiting just around the corner.

Aim high. Send examples of your CV to the personnel officers of companies you would like to work for. You've got nothing to lose in trying.

Apply for seasonal jobs in the summer. Hotels, holiday camps, funfairs, and theme parks all take on extra staff for July and August. Many of them prefer mature, experienced staff who are accustomed to handling people.

Look at advertisements for voluntary workers in your neighborhood. There are all sorts of organizations that need you—for driving patients to hospital, working in charity shops, or being a guide in local churches and public buildings.

All voluntary organizations (and many commercial ones) are always looking for skilled fundraisers. If you have skills in this direction, you will be able to pick and choose for whom you work.

If you are mechanically-minded, consider buying, renovating, and selling on cars. Start with a single vehicle. Look at local advertisements, and consult trade guides to ascertain a sensible resale price.

Add a touch of glamour to your life. If you live near a film or television studio, become an extra in crowd scenes. Beware: the hours are long and the day starts early!

Turn adversity to your benefit. "Although I love gardening, I never had a real one of my own. Now I have five! I put a card in a shop window offering my services as a part-time gardener, and I was overwhelmed with responses."
RETIRED OFFICE WORKER

Take setbacks in your stride.

Believe in what you are doing. The playwright Tennessee Williams wrote some outstanding plays and a number of flops. He kept on writing because, as he said, "It means freedom of being, and if you can't be yourself what's the point of being anything at all?"

Leave your job on a high. If your company doesn't give you a farewell party, throw one of your own.

Don't wind down in your final months at work. People tend to remember their last impressions of colleagues. Go out on top form, being as productive and useful as ever.

If you want your job to taper off gradually, ask if you can work part-time for a few months before retirement.

Use your office farewell party as an occasion to make arrangements to keep in touch with former colleagues in the future. Exchange telephone numbers and e-mail addresses.

When making a farewell speech, be positive and funny, and don't pay off old scores in public.

Unless you're returning to work, don't go back to your former workplace in office hours, hoping for a gossip. Move on—you are in a new phase of your life where you should be looking forward and not back.

Embrace retirement. Don't brood about your former workplace. On your first day without work, go out somewhere pleasant for the day with your partner or friend, as a distraction.

Timetable a short period of relaxation for each day. Let no one disturb you and allow yourself to indulge in some me-time.

Start attending school and college reunions you have been too busy to go to. You will enjoy widening your horizons by meeting up with old friends, and you may make useful contacts.

Be enthusiastic. If you're going to do what you want to do, do it with gusto and enjoyment.

Cull your wardrobe. Be realistic. There are some clothes that will have dated or will probably never fit you again no matter how much exercise you take.

Try to shop for new clothes at least once a year, to give you a smart, up-to-date appearance. Remember: first appearances count.

Alternatively, if you really don't want to embrace sartorial change, stand fast, on the principle that what goes around comes around. If you never change your dress style, you stand a chance of being in the forefront of fashion at least twice in your lifetime!

Dress in what suits you, not what you think you should wear. Today, thanks to exercise and diet, many sixty-year-olds are in better shape than their grown-up children.

Consider changing your car. Web sites will give you an idea of sensible discounts to which to aspire. Use these as the basis for haggling.

In any forward planning, always remember the great acronym S. K. I.—Spend the Kids' Inheritance.

Start shopping at off-peak hours. It might give you an altogether pleasanter view of stores and malls.

Put your experience or interests to good use by becoming a lunchtime or after-dinner speaker. Local organizations and clubs are desperate for enthusiasts to address them about their hobbies or experiences. There are generally no fees, but you will meet plenty of people and get a lot of free meals.

Consider entering local politics. There is no telling where this may lead. Former movie star Ronald Reagan was in his mid-fifties when he became Governor of California en route to becoming President of the USA.

Embrace competition—it encourages you to better yourself.

Redecorate your home to mark your retirement, taking into account the therapeutic effects of different colors. Black, gray, and brown are neutral colors. Red, orange, and yellow are warm, energizing colors. Blue, violet, and green are cool, restful colors.

Become a poet. Greeting card companies are on the lookout for fresh talent in this area.

Join a circus. All over the world there are schools and academies specializing in training circus acts. You may be a little mature to learn a high-wire routine, but think of the fun you could have devising a specialty act to appeal to the over-sixties!

Become a local historian. John McNamara worked for the New York Housing Authority for almost thirty-nine years, but he spent every spare moment walking the streets of his neighborhood, the Bronx. He also used canoes and kayaks to cover all the waterways in the area. After his sixtieth birthday he published a definitive history of the Bronx called *History in Asphalt*.

Invent something—now's the perfect time to develop any ingenious ideas you've ever had.

Develop your own philosophy and live by it. See if you can sway others to live by it, too.

at home
and abroad

Think about moving home.
If you move to a smaller,
more manageable house, you
could realize a profit that
will help in your retirement.

Visit the Christ of the Andes statue
in the Uspallata Pass on the border
between Argentina and Chile. This
bronze statue of Christ is 26 feet
tall; he has one hand on a cross
and the other raised in blessing.
In 1904, the statue was dedicated
to peace between the two nations.

Give something back to the environment after all these years of using its resources: devote the next few years to building a home that is eco-friendly, and incorporate natural materials.

If you have the expertise—and the stamina—join a self-build group. A group of specialists—such as builders, plumbers, electricians— buy a plot of land and with their combined expertise, build houses for the members of the group.

If you are planning to move to a new location, pamper yourself. Look for an area with a climate that you will thrive in.

Think about moving into a sheltered housing complex, which is normally reserved for those over fifty-five. These usually have a resident warden, and sometimes include restaurants and facilities for suitable recreational activities.

Be a good neighbor. Welcome new arrivals to your street with freshly baked cookies or a plant.

Visit Lourdes, which is situated at the foot of the Pyrenees, in France. It is the birthplace of St. Bernadette. In 1858, the Virgin Mary appeared before Bernadette in a vision. Today, many sick people visit Lourdes on pilgrimages of healing.

When you move, remember that you will have to put in some effort to get to know other folks. Relish this opportunity to gain a whole new social circle.

Whether you are moving house or staying put, declutter! Be very selective about the possessions you retain and clear out accumulated junk, but keep those items that truly reflect your personality.

The pace of life is slower in the country. Decide whether you hanker after peace and quiet after a lifetime living in a vibrant city.

Thinking of making the big move and living abroad? Use the time before retirement to take trial vacations in the country in question then try to spend at least three consecutive months there.

Learn a language. If you are keen to live abroad one day, you'll be delighted to be able to communicate with the locals. In any case, speaking another language is a useful skill to have and a fantastic excuse to go abroad on vacation.

Visit the two temples of Ramses II and his wife Nefertari in Egypt. These were constructed in the thirteenth century B.C., but in 1964, they were threatened by the waters of the new High Dam at Aswan. To ensure their safety, they were dismantled and then rebuilt, block by block, 200 feet up the face of a cliff.

Look into doing some sort of work from home after you retire. In the US alone, more than 25 million people operate home-based businesses. Many of these businesses are set up by people aged between fifty and sixty, to be operated full-time after retirement.

If you'd like to run a home-based business, check whether your present home is suitable. The three basic businesses usually run from home are providing services, manufacturing objects, and selling, each of which require different facilities.

If you are setting up a business at home, situate the business area of your house apart from the living area. Try to create a balance and harmony between the two areas. Organize a separate telephone line for your business.

Get out and about. "Without new experiences something inside of us sleeps."
FRANK HERBERT

Go traveling with your partner and have an adventure.

When you're on vacation, get off the beaten track. Be a real traveler, not a tourist.

Go to the Taj Mahal mausoleum at Agra in India, one of the most beautiful buildings in the world. It was erected on the orders of Emperor Shah Jahan, in memory of his wife, the empress, and work on it started in 1631. It is built on the banks of the River Yamuna.

Take a trip on the most isolated and least frequented rail journey you can find. Shut your eyes and imagine that you are traveling on the Orient Express.

A sea cruise may afford the vacation of a lifetime. There are many to choose from and some are relatively inexpensive. Don't sign up unless you are reasonably convivial—you are going to be stuck with your fellow passengers for days, or even weeks.

Instead of flying or driving to a vacation destination, go on a bus tour. Bus travel is an excellent way of holidaying in your sixties. Modern buses are very comfortable and take the stress out of travel.

Before you set off on vacation, make it a rule to study the culture of the area you are going to visit, as well as the geography.

Relax on your travels.
"A middle-aged person has likely learned to have a little fun in spite of his troubles."
Don Marquis

Don't let age deter you from going anywhere. The Danish explorer Vitus Bering was sixty when he embarked upon his last great voyage.

You are now approaching the age at which you can put your experience, thinking, and reading to good use by contemplating and refining your philosophy of life. Try to visit at least one famous shrine in the world. Enjoy its beauty and historical associations, and spend some time there in contemplation.

Visit the Sengakuji temple in Minato-ku, Tokyo, Japan. It is a shrine to the forty-seven ronin *who avenged the death of their master but were put to death themselves. This could be a suitable shrine at which to consider the virtues of service and loyalty.*

Take a lodger and put that spare room to good use.

Go to the Chapel of Grace at Kevelaer in Germany. In 1641, Hendrick Busman, a merchant visiting a roadside cross, heard a voice, three times, telling him to build a chapel there. He did so. For centuries, there has been a famous pilgrimage from the city of Bonn to the Chapel of Grace. It covers 65 miles and occupies eight days.

Take a trip to Canterbury Cathedral in Kent, England. It was at Canterbury in the year 597 that St. Augustine baptized King Ethelbert and began to spread Christianity throughout Britain.

Delve into history and create a reconstruction of a building you admire.

Visit Uluru National Park (formerly Ayers Rock) in Australia. This is a huge colored rock growing out of a red, sandy plain in the Northern Territory. Uluru is an area of great cultural and religious significance to the aboriginal people and is a beautiful place to visit.

Dabble in do-it-yourself. Make a bookshelf or something even more adventurous that you can showcase in your home.

Link up and travel with young people from time to time. Temple University in Philadelphia formed an improvisational drama company called The Full Circle. It consisted of ten students and ten people over fifty. The group toured very successfully, putting on plays about the generation gap.

ambitions
and goals

Don't constrict yourself with time limits. Just get on and do whatever it is that you want to do and enjoy it.

Break down each ambition into component parts. Use a checklist as you achieve each section. If you want to fly a plane, join an airfield, or book your first lesson.

Take advice, but don't let it interfere with your plans. You are old enough to know your own mind by now.

Be prepared to make sacrifices to fulfill your ambitions if necessary.

If you crave your fifteen minutes of fame, now is the time to make one last bid for stardom—apply to a reality TV show.

Be single-minded. Politely repel time-wasters and those who tell you that you can't do things. It's your life and your future.

Take your time as you pursue an ambition. As you reach each staging post, stop and take time to do other things. It's good to enjoy the journey and the view on the way up.

Pay off your mortgage as soon as you can afford it. The feeling of relief is wonderful.

Don't worry about stress. You probably experienced plenty of that at work when you were not in charge of what happened. Now you are in command of your life.

Plan to start retirement with a bang. Decide on a spectacular "one-off" experience you have always wanted to try—a glider flight, a day on a famous golf course, a bungee-jump—and find out how you can do it. If retirement is looming, make the reservation for the very first day of your retirement, to show yourself that you are serious about making the most of the next decades.

Attack all of your plans with confidence and optimism.

Visualize what you want to do. Savor that vision and really think it through before proceeding.

Be ambitious. Everything that you are going to do now is for you. And those lucky enough to accompany you, of course. Live by the doctrine that it is never too late.

Abraham Lincoln once said, "Every man is said to have his peculiar ambition." Pursue your ambitions even if they seem unusual to others; they're yours.

Stick to your goals but be prepared to change direction if necessary—the more flexible and adaptable you are, the more likely it is that you will seek out different or unexpected paths to success.

Don't worry if you think you don't have as much natural talent as others. The great Albert Einstein said that he was no genius, but that he possessed the essential qualities of curiosity, obsession, endurance, and self-criticism.

Don't complain.
Remember that
most remedies lie
in your hands.

Consider developing any skills you have. You now have time to become a better musician, improve your skiing ability, and so on.

Don't be too proud to accept help if it is offered. Just because you're older, it doesn't always mean that you are wiser.

You can reach the top of your profession after you're sixty. The experience and information you have picked up over the years are invaluable.

*Congratulate yourself constantly. Remind
yourself of what you have achieved already
and use this to spur you on to greater things.*

Consider a career change—you're never
too old. Dwight D. Eisenhower, the
Allied Supreme Commander in World
War II, had never shown any great
interest in politics. Yet in the 1950s, he
accepted the Republican nomination for
President of the USA and (past his
sixtieth birthday) won by a large
majority; he was re-elected in 1956.

Use what you have learned through
your life and work experience to
better your experiences from here
on out. Never stop learning.

Keep your eyes open for business opportunities. You are now in a much better position to dedicate time and energy to making a proposition work.

Celebrate change—you can't stop it from happening so you may as well embrace it.

Whatever you want to do, go for it! If you don't try it now, you probably never will and you'll spend the rest of your life regretting your decision.

Enlist the support of your partner and family before embarking on any change.

If you are happy where you are, don't change. The great popular composer, Irving Berlin, never learned to play the piano properly, although he wrote thousands of tunes. When he approached what would be the retiring age for most people, he decided against taking piano lessons. "I figured that in the time it took me to learn I could have written a few songs and made myself some money," he commented.

Be in control. Ignore enforced reasons for making a change. It is your life and you are in charge of it.

Draw upon your own experiences and use them in your grand plan. The great American primitive artist, Anna "Grandma" Moses, was in her seventies when she started painting, using memories of her farming background from the 1860s to produce such paintings as Catching the Thanksgiving Turkey. She painted on flat boards in her bedroom and developed an international reputation.

Tinker to your heart's content.

If you have one good idea, spend time perfecting it.

If you are trying to break into print, think about writing a local guide, which will have a guaranteed appeal for residents and visitors alike.

If you've always wanted to be a writer, start by writing letters to your local newspaper. You probably won't get paid, but it's all good experience. Work your way up to sending letters or short stories to national magazines. Many of these pay quite well.

Keep a scrapbook of articles that you enjoyed reading and which have inspired you. Refer to them if you ever need encouragement to write some of your own material.

Always wanted to write a book? Write a synopsis and three specimen chapters. You can approach publishers yourself, but you may have a better chance of success if you can get an agent to represent you.

Don't let a lack of qualifications put you off doing anything.

Consider publishing your own book. First work out if you think there will be a market for it. Sometimes a history of a local sports team will find buyers among fans. If you write one of these, try to arrange for the club store of your local team to stock it.

Set up a Web site and create an online community.

Don't be afraid to go it alone if you have to.

Start your own "Where are they now?" list. See if you can trace any heroes—or villains—of your youth.

Have you always felt strongly about something? Now is the time to launch a campaign to achieve your objectives—better street lighting, safer road crossings, and so on. Write a letter to the local newspaper or radio station, gather publicity, arrange a meeting, and get local politicians on your side.

Go national, or even global. Join a national or international organization, such as the Gray Panthers, which represents your interests.

Stand up and speak out.

love and romance

Be grateful for what you've had—and still have.

> "Immature love says, 'I love you because I need you.' Mature love says, 'I need you because I love you.'"
>
> ERICH FROMM

Don't let a day go by without doing something positive for a loved one. Remember that love can last forever if you want it to and are prepared to keep the flame burning.

Work long and hard at your love and it will work for you.

Weather the bad times—a period of transition can put some strain on even the steadiest of partnerships. The closer the bond you have, the better your chance of weathering any stress.

Start making your plans for the future together, at least two or three years before your retirement. Book that round-the-world trip now so that you have something to look forward to.

Don't place too many demands on your partner.

Concentrate on your partner's good points—and tell them what they are.

If you haven't before because one or both of you was working, agree to share household chores (or better yet, get a cleaner!)

Find a silly habit or hobby that you and your partner can enjoy as a couple. Put on old records on a Sunday afternoon and dance like you are teenagers again, or take up pottery classes together.

Go with your partner to a bar and pretend you don't know each other. Flirt with each other as if for the first time.

Make plans with your partner. Discuss your individual and joint ambitions well in advance. Talk frankly about your hopes and fears.

Arrange to do some things together, but also make plans for individual activities, so that you have your own lives and so remain interesting to one another.

Encourage one another in your personal ambitions and show faith in your choices.

Tolerate each other's hobbies. John Harrison, a humble British watchmaker, spent most of his life trying to perfect a marine chronometer that would transform navigation at sea by determining longitude accurately. In the process, he turned his small house into a virtual workshop. His second wife put up with the chaos for decades. Harrison was over sixty before his chronometer finally worked and he was awarded a large cash prize by Parliament.

Make plans and stick to them. House-selling is said to be about "location, location, location." A happy retirement together is all about "priorities, priorities, priorities."

Exchange wish lists.

Tread warily. When you and your partner retire, it can take some time to adjust when you are at both at home full-time.

Introduce your partner to some of your interests. Go to the theater or an art gallery together.

Take the time to create a family album. It's good to revisit and share your memories.

Timetable the use of the family car (or better yet, buy another!)

Share the television remote control.

Respect your partner's privacy. If you have the space, use separate rooms in the house for your hobbies and activities.

*Have friends in common
and make more friends as
a couple, but don't be afraid
to have individual friends,
especially if you are pursuing
interests of your own.*

Don't criticize one another's friends.

Put aside a time each week in which to talk to your partner in depth. Be completely open about your feelings and aspirations.

Listen to each other. "It takes two to speak the truth—one to speak, and another to hear."

HENRY DAVID THOREAU

If you're single, take advantage of specialized dating agencies. Know that 16 percent of people signing up to Internet dating agencies are aged fifty-five and over—the fastest growing age group to enroll.

Be proactive about dating. Members of your age group tend to be more clear-headed and practical. They are often better at dating than younger people, because they are more at ease in social situations.

Be optimistic. More than one in five singles over the age of fifty-five believes that they will find romance within a year.

Tread carefully.
"I never deny,
I never contradict,
I sometimes forget."
BENJAMIN DISRAELI

Forget how old you are.
"Spring still makes spring in the mind,
When sixty years are told:
Love makes anew this throbbing heart
And we are never old."

RALPH WALDO EMERSON

There is hope, there is romance and, above all, there is Viagra.

Don't give up sex for Lent, in
case you can't get started again.

Rent the movies *On Golden Pond*, *Mrs. Miniver*, and *Random Harvest*, and watch them regularly together. They are the best depictions of mature love ever put on film.

Stick together.
"Grow old along with me!
The best is yet to be."
ROBERT BROWNING

Appreciate that love does not follow a calendar and pays no attention to age. "Love, all alike, no season knows,
    nor clime,
nor hours, days, months, which are the
    rags of time."
JOHN DONNE

Go on a second honeymoon. Research shows that they are generally cheaper than the first—about $2,700 compared with $3,200!

Celebrate your wedding anniversary by renewing your marriage vows. Look back over your marriage and choose a venue or location that has meant a lot to you both over the years.

Always celebrate your wedding anniversaries in style. Take a trip together or go out for a special meal and remind yourselves of how much you mean to each other.

Prepare and hang on the wall a calendar showing all the days that have become special to you both since you first met—the birth of children and grandchildren, journeys undertaken, etc.

Treasure the knowledge that the older you get, the more memories you will have. "What greater thing is there for two human souls than to feel that they are joined... to strengthen one another."

GEORGE ELIOT

In exactly sixty words, write down why you love your partner. Give this list to your partner.

Give your partner a windowbox with
lots of different seed varieties planted
in it. Throw away the packets so neither
of you knows which flowers to expect.
A good, lasting marriage has its pleasant
uncertainties as well.

*Share financial problems
with your partner.*

Persevere. Research shows that many marriages improve later in life. This is due to a number of things, including improvement of financial circumstances, the consequent lessening of stress and, above all, improved communication.

Have confidence in your partner as your marriage continues to last into your sixties. This will enable you to be yourself and also to grow and develop within your marriage or partnership.

If you're not in a relationship, don't give up on love. Keep searching—you'll be glad you did.

Treasure love at sixty. Spoil your partner and let them know frequently how much they mean to you with words and gifts.

> Young love is a flame; very pretty, often very hot and fierce, but still only light and flickering. The love of the older and disciplined heart is as coals, deep burning, unquenchable.
>
> HENRY WARD BEECHER

Give your partner an unexpected gift to symbolize your pleasure in your long marriage. It could be a garland of flowers, or something similar, to represent the binding tie.

Appreciate and respond to the fact that your partner will change and develop over your years together.

" A successful marriage requires falling in love many times, always with the same person. "
MIGNON MCLAUGHLIN

Nurture your love slowly. See if there are things that you can find out about your partner at the age of sixty that you never knew before. "Love seems the swiftest, but it is the slowest of all growths. No man or woman knows what perfect love is until they have been married a quarter of a century."

MARK TWAIN

An Hachette Company
First Published in Great Britain in 2005 by Spruce,
a division of Octopus Publishing Company Ltd
2–4 Heron Quays, London E14 4JP.
www.octopusbooks.co.uk
www.octopusbooksusa.com

Distributed in the U.S. and Canada for Octopus Books USA
c/- Hachette Book Group USA
237 Park Avenue
New York NY 10017.

Copyright © Octopus Publishing Group Ltd, 2005, 2008
Text © Graeme Kent 2005
Illustrations © Robyn Neild 2005

Graeme Kent asserts the moral right to be identified as the author of this book.

ISBN: 978-1-84072-810-1

5 7 9 0 8 6 4

Printed and bound in China.

31901046441236